FLYING RADIO CONTROL AEROBATICS

Other titles in this series include:

Flying
Radio Control
Aerobatics

Charles Allison & Andy Nicholls

ARGUS BOOKS

Argus Books
Argus House
Boundary Way
Hemel Hempstead
Hertfordshire HP2 7ST
England

First published by Argus Books 1990

© Argus Books 1990

ISBN 1 85486 018 6

Phototypesetting by GCS, Leighton Buzzard
Printed and bound in Great Britain by
William Clowes Ltd, Beccles

Contents

ABOUT THE CO-AUTHOR

Andy Nicholls started in aerobatic competitions in 1986 and in 1989 became the British and GBRCAA Champion. He represented the United Kingdom at the European Championships in 1988, and at the World Championships in 1989. He has been selected for the 1990 European Championships. This book is based on the knowledge, skills and experience gained by Andy during this period.

Acknowledgements

MILLER'S RADIO MODELS (who kindly built and finished the control model)
2B, The Parade,
Tattenham Way,
Burgh Heath.
Tadworth Surrey Tel. 0737 363176

SOLAR FILM (who kindly supplied the covering materials)
Solar film was used to cover the model.

RIPMAX MODELS (who kindly supplied the kit, engine, radio gear and decorfilm)
Green Street
Enfield EN3 7SJ

Distributers of Futaba Radio Control Equipment
ENYA engines
Mick Reeves GANGSTER kits
Decorfilm adhesive trim

BRITISH MODEL FLYING ASSOCIATION (BMFA)
Checksfield House
31, St. Andrews Road
Leicester LE2 8RE Tel. 0533 440028

GREAT BRITAIN RADIO CONTROL AEROBATIC ASSOCIATION (GBRCAA)
Contact the BMFA for the address of the current secretary.

Chapter 1
Introduction

AEROBATICS is the tracing of set shapes in a predefined area of the sky. This area is called the *box* and it is placed at a distance of approximately 150 metres from the pilot. Its size is measured in degrees from where the pilot stands. The horizontal (A-axis) limits are 60 degrees either side of a centre line. The upper vertical limit is 60 degrees above the ground and the lower, although not actually specified, is about 15 degrees from the ground and is

called the base line. Although most manoeuvres are flown along the A-axis, there are some which are flown at 90 degrees to that axis. This line is known as the B-axis, and there are no specific limits other than the need to keep at approximately 150 metres.

Flying competitive aerobatics introduces new disciplines, the most significant of which is that each manoeuvre must be followed by the next as specified in the schedule. No longer can you exit a manoeuvre at the wrong attitude and choose a manoeuvre which matches that exit. If the schedule requires a square loop to follow a half reverse cuban eight, then that is the way it must be flown.

The other key point is that every schedule requires extensive use of the rudder and its effect on the model at different speeds and attitudes has to be mastered.

If you are to enjoy aerobatics, it is vital that you first achieve a reasonable degree of confidence and ability in flying low-wing models using aileron, elevator

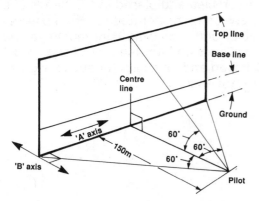

The aerobatic box.

and rudder, and be capable of handling models at high speeds. It would be to your advantage to have passed the BMFA A and B certificates, as they provide an early introduction to disciplined flying and may be a requirement when entering competitions.

If you intend to achieve a reasonable standard, a certain amount of commitment is necessary, and practice and more practice in all kinds of weather and wind strengths will become the order of the day. The reward of being able to fly graceful aerobatic manoeuvres may seem enough in itself, but there is also the added challenge of progressing through the various standards of competence, competing for a place in the National team and then against the top pilots from all nations. It does not stop there, as there are many opportunities to fly demonstrations at various shows ranging from the local model club through local/county shows to national and international events.

The sport is controlled by the Federation Aeronautique Internationale (FAI). In the United Kingdom, the Great Britain Radio Controlled Aerobatic Association (GBRCAA) is the representative body which organises competitions all over the country from April to October. The membership fee is minimal and regular newsletters are published, which give useful information on all aspects of model aerobatic flying and the latest updates on the progress of the sport.

There are three levels of competence. Newcomers to the GBRCAA start with the Standard Schedule, which this book addresses. Progression to the Senior and the full FAI (Master) schedules is achieved by gaining sufficient points in two separate events within a twelve month period.

The BMFA also runs a series of 'centralised' events which are open to all members of the BMFA. These competitions are run in conjunction with the GBRCAA. The annual highlight is the National Championship, which is usually held over the August Bank Holiday weekend, where over 40 pilots may compete for this coveted title.

The purpose of this book is to give the newcomer an overall view of the ways in which a model, engine and radio equipment can be chosen. It includes a detailed description of how to trim the model, tackle the basic components which make up aerobatic manoeuvres and then attempt the full Standard Schedule. There are pointers on how the controls should be used to allow for a prevailing wind condition, and possible down grades that could affect every manoeuvre. Finally, there is information on the organisation of competitions and the approach of judges.

To validate the contents of this book, a readily available low-cost combination of model, radio and engine was assembled and placed in the hands of a newcomer to aerobatics. His observations and criticisms contributed to the final version. A summary of the model chosen and its characteristics are given in Appendix 1.

Chapter 2
Choosing a model

EVEN EXPERIENCED aerobatic fliers find that although some models are to their liking, others they cannot adjust to and rarely will they keep the same model for a third season. There are many so-called aerobatic models on the market, but they are really no more than sports aerobatic models which, although they will fly the manoeuvres, are not as precise as models specifically designed for the purpose.

The elusive perfect aerobatic model will fly as straight as an arrow in any attitude over a wide range of throttle settings, have just enough drag to check it in downward manoeuvres but with enough performance to climb vertically for ever. Its roll rate will be crisp and not laboured, stall turns will be majestic and not flicked wingovers, corners will be pulled tight or open with constant radii to suit the manoeuvre, and so on. Does it exist? Who really knows? What does matter, however, is that you understand the characteristics of an aerobatic model and its capabilities, and are able to build, assemble and trim it so that the aerobatic characteristics designed into the model are not lost.

First and foremost it is *not* necessary to start with a top-of-the-range model powered by a pumped 60 motor with a tuned pipe, in-flight mixture control and retracts. While all or some of these may be considered essential by the top-rated fliers, the beginner can learn aerobatics with a lesser model powered by an unpumped motor with standard exhaust, no in-flight mix and fitted with a fixed undercarriage.

In aerobatic competitions, the models are flown at a distance of approximately one hundred and fifty metres from the judges and must therefore be of sufficient size to be clearly visible. There will be times, for example in severe crosswinds, when the model is pushed much further away. In general, wingspans of between sixty and seventy inches are used. The completed model should have as light a wing loading as possible and probably weigh between seven and half and eight and a half pounds. A very light model will be more affected by turbulence, while a heavier model will lack vertical performance and crispness in flight.

Having said this, there is no reason why the beginner should not start with a smaller and lighter model and that is why a Gangster 63 was chosen as the control model to support this book.

The FAI rules for the F3A class state the maximum surface area allowed is 150dm², and the maximum total weight is 5kg.

The fuselage

It is essential that the fuselage is *absolutely* straight without the slightest hint that it has even seen a banana, otherwise it will not fly straight and the model will require constant in-flight correction. Many would-be aerobats could improve their scores dramatically if they acquired a true model. If you are building your own model, use a jig and double-check the wood, etc., to make sure it is true and of consistent quality. Manufacturers do their best to ensure that their kits are properly quality controlled but, even so, it is still possible for a rogue piece of material to slip through. Don't hesitate to replace anything you are not happy with. You only build the model once, so it is best to get it right at the outset rather than have to try to correct any building defect later on.

Another point to consider is that the

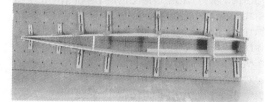

The use of a jig helps in the building of a straight fuselage. *(Photo: Tim Allison)*

The engine mount is offset to the left with right side thrust to ensure the prop. driver lies on the fuselage centre line. *(Photo: Tim Allison)*

amount of side and downthrust may need to be adjusted during the trimming phase. Assuming you have no other information to hand, build in side and downthrust in accordance with instructions, but do make sure there is enough room to allow the engine to be repositioned to give up to, say 7 degrees of right sidethrust and 3 degrees of downthrust without requiring a major rebuild of the cowling. Although this amount of sidethrust may well seem extreme, it will be necessary if you want your model to fly vertical lines without it veering off to the left. On some models it may be best to leave the completion and finishing of the front of the model until the optimum thrust settings have been determined.

The wings

Aerobatic models have symmetrical wings and will probably spend as much time flying inverted as they do upright. It does not matter too much if it is a low or mid-wing model. The advantage of a low wing is that it will probably provide more space within the fuselage for the radio, etc., but a mid-wing will enable a tuned pipe to be partially or fully cowled, which improves the model's appearance

This model has an upright engine with the tuned pipe enclosed in the top of the fuselage—European Championships, Sweden, 1988. *(Photo: A. Nicholls)*

and can contribute to a reduction in noise levels.

Wings are generally made from obechi or balsa veneered styro foam but there is nothing to stop you from using built-up wings which could be lighter but will probably take a little more time to build accurately. Before joining the wing halves, check to make sure each half matches the other and there are no obvious warps, that the chords at the root and tips are the same and that you do, in fact, have a *left* and *right* wing. Then draw a line through the centreline of the tip of each wing and pin a piece of rectangular balsa of sufficient height to raise the wing tip by the amount required for the dihedral. Then place the wings on a *flat* horizontal surface (check it with a spirit level) and dry join the

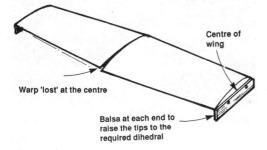

Warp 'lost' at the centre

Centre of wing

Balsa at each end to raise the tips to the required dihedral

Aligning the wings to 'lose' any slight warp at the centre.

wings at the roots. The purpose of this is to lose any warps at the centre for, if they are aligned at the centre the wings will have twisted tips requiring aileron trim to maintain level flight. If there is more than two or three millimetres difference, then consider getting another set.

Sand the wing roots to butt-join them at the correct dihedral angle. Glue with epoxy and reinforce the joint in the usual way with fibreglass bandage and polyester or epoxy resin. The chances are that the dihedral suggested in the instructions may not be exactly right and it is only possible to determine whether the dihedral angle is correct by flying and trimming the model. If the dihedral needs to be adjusted, saw through the top wing and either cut out some foam if the dihedral is to be increased or insert a balsa wedge if the dihedral is too great, and finish it as before.

Retractable undercarriage

Retracts are ideal for a tarmac-type runway but the legs do tend to get bent on grass strips, and often need to be straightened after each landing to ensure they align with their recess holes. Retracts add a little to the all-up weight but, when retracted, reduce drag and present a nicer profile in flight. However, they add to the cost and to the building time, and require an additional servo(s) to operate them. They are by no means vital to begin with, but the serious competitors will invariably use them.

There are two main types available, mechanical and pneumatic. Mechanical ones require a servo to operate and lock the retract mechanism. Should the undercarriage become jammed, thus stalling the retract servo, a separate battery is recommended to avoid draining the main battery used for other functions.

Pneumatic retracts operate on compressed air regulated by a servo-operated valve to raise or lower the legs. The air is stored in a small high-pressure tank which is merely pumped up before each flight with a bicycle or high-pressure pump.

The choice of tricycle or tail-dragger undercarriages will probably depend on the model design. However, given a choice, it is worth noting that a tail dragger set up does not interfere with the positioning of the tuned pipe on an inverted rear exhaust set up.

Control linkages

Positive and precise control over each control surface is essential if accurate flying is to be achieved. There must be minimum gap between the control surfaces and that part of the model to which they are attached. Use good quality hinges/mylar strip and peg them. Consider using a closed loop system for the rudder to prevent blow back, and Y-ended pushrods to each side of the elevator for evenness of movement and adjustment on both sides. Use separate servos for each aileron linked by a Y-lead or electronic mixing if the transmitter has this facility. This will give more positive control and reliability in the event of a servo failure. It will also help in achieving differential movement when trimming the model.

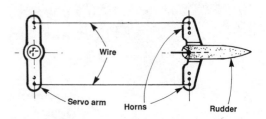

Principle of the closed loop for the rudder. The wires, servo arm and horns should form a parallelogram.

Alignment of the fin and wings

This is a critical phase of the building, and time spent now in ensuring correct alignment will be rewarded later. It must not be rushed—be prepared to spend an hour or two to get it right. The time and care taken to build a straight fuselage and wings will be wasted if the fin is not truly vertical to the fuselage, the tailplane is not at exactly 90 degrees to the fin and fuselage, and similarly for the wings. A flat surface, a long steel rule, and twine with no, or very little, elasticity are essential, as is a good eye and, perhaps, a second opinion. The points for alignment are best shown in the diagram.

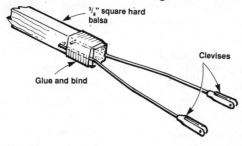

'Y' rod for the elevator.

Ensure that the fin is truly vertical and the tailplane is at 90° to it. (Photo: Tim Allison)

12

Checking the alignment.

Finishing

Covering the model can be time-consuming but a nicely finished model is a joy to own and fly. It is not intended that this book should advise on the many options available but, whatever method you choose, bear in mind that you must always be able to see the wingtips and so make sure you do not leave them white. It is generally best to paint the fuselage and film the wing and tailplane..

A quick but professional and attractive design can be easily achieved by using adhesive Decorfilm.

Acquiring a model

Once you have fixed your budget, there are several approaches. Much will depend on timescale, confidence in your own building ability, availability of kits etc.

Second-hand models

Buying a second-hand model will allow you to begin flying quickly and there may even be the chance of a test flight before you buy. Apart from the advantage of getting airborne straight away, you should be able to find out about some of the model's characteristics from its previous owner. It is, of course, difficult to change the alignment of components on a completed model without a major rebuild. It is unlikely that you will discover a top notch aerobatic model up for sale, but any of the popular sport aerobatic designs will at least allow you to learn some of the fundamentals of flying aerobatics. Prices

This model has an inverted four stroke engine and air brakes on the retractable under-carriage legs—European Championships, Sweden, 1988.
(Photo: A. Nicholls)

usually compare quite favourably with the equivalent kit price, taking into account construction costs and time.

Almost-ready-to-fly-models

Almost-ready-to-fly models also offer a quick route to getting airborne. They are generally proven fliers and their characteristics are known and publicised. The penalty may be in their seemingly high price and the slight possibility that the fuselage or wings may be warped. If building time, cost of glues and covering materials, etc., are taken into account, the price of such models is probably not so excessive after all!

The EZ range of kits such as the Suprafly have achieved high placings at competitions.

Kits

Kits are varied and plentiful and come in a range of prices to suit your pocket. The quality of kits can vary considerably, and at the end of the day you generally get what you pay for. This is where the advice you can get from a good model shop can be invaluable. Depending on the amount of pre-fabrication, you must be prepared to spend several evenings building but do you have control over the accuracy of building. The Joker, Dalotel, Challenger, etc., from Dave Smith Models, all represent good value and have performed well in recent years.

Plans and plan-packs

Plans of top aerobatic models occasionally become available. The cost of parts may be less than if bought with a kit, and you will have the opportunity of selecting every piece of timber yourself. Some models are available as plan-packs which include such items as canopy, cowling, foam wings and tailplane and plan.

Own-design

Own-design is best left until you have tried a few different aerobatic models. You need to be able to identify what it was about them which caused you to want to try something else, and then be able to correct those faults in the design of your own machine. This approach has the potential of offering the greatest reward in sense of achievement and in

This model has an inverted engine and a fixed undercarriage— European Championships, Sweden, 1988. *(Photo: A. Nicholls)*

owning a model that is unique. However, be warned—it is time-consuming, and there is always the possibility that when the model eventually takes to the air it may not be what you thought you had built!

Andy Nicholls' first own-design model—the Illusion—took many hours to design and build. He had to learn new techniques, such as mould-making for the canopy and cowl including GRP moulding techniques. The sense of achievement and satisfaction when it flew for the first time was tremendous and words alone cannot describe it. Only a minimum of trimming was needed and it has since placed well in national and international competitions.

Andy Nicholls with his own design *Illusion.*
(*Photo: Tim Allison*)

Chapter 3
Choosing an engine

THE F3A CLASS for aerobatics allows engines up to .60cu.in. (10cc) for two-strokes, and 1.20cu.in. (20cc) for four-strokes. For this engine size there are many variations in design and construction from the same and different manufacturers. Various combinations of materials for piston, bore and liner—such as ABC or AAC (A for Aluminium, B for Bronze and C for Chrome)—give improved performance. Long-stroke engines have an advantage in that they will turn propellers with a larger diameter and increased pitch, thereby giving greater performance at a reduced RPM and so reducing propeller noise. The choice of a side or rear exhaust engine may be governed by the design of the model but, in general, a rear exhaust allows for a tidier and easier installation.

There is no central control over the measurement of the bhp ratings and probably, at the end of the day, your best advice will come from observing and comparing the performance of various engines. You may find it interesting to note that, at a competition, a pilot attached a spring balance to the tailwheel of various models and discovered that it was *not* the highest rated bhps, as given by the manufacturers, which produced the most static thrust. Before you discount any engine through apparent poor performance, make sure that it was set up properly with the right propeller, plug and exhaust system.

There is nothing to be gained by opting for a smaller model and putting in the biggest (and thereby, perhaps, the heaviest) and most powerful engine you can lay your hands on. The engine must suit the airframe and this combination be capable of being properly trimmed out without sacrificing any of the features designed into it.

Pumped motors

Pumped motors are generally preferred because they offer a constant supply of fuel to the carburettor regardless of the attitude of the model. This is particularly important when flying ascending vertical manoeuvres. There should be no hint of fuel starvation when flying unlimited vertical climbs.

It is worth noting that, because of the high performance of current pumped engines, the rear bearings tend to require replacing quite frequently. Many articles have been written on the subject of bearing wear, and the consensus of opinion seems to be that they are too small for the immense workload placed upon them. The design of the engine influences the ease with which bearings can be changed, and some are relatively simple as the rear bearing is mounted on the rear of the front housing and easily accessed. In time, if you can afford it, consider having two engines, one for practice and one for use in competitions.

Fuel

There are various castor and synthetic based fuels on the market containing varying percentages of nitromethane (or its equivalent). An increase in the percentage of nitro will produce an improvement in the smoothness of throttle response and top-end performance. Remember that, if your engine has a tuned pipe, its length should be shortened if the percentage of nitro is increased to give higher revs (and vice versa). Percentages can vary from nil to 20% and it is a matter of experiment to find out which produces the best performance. Always filter the fuel through a muslin filter when you transfer it into the fuel container, and include a fuel filter in the supply to the tank.

Plugs

Plugs affect performance and reliability.

Generally, lower percentages of nitro require a hotter (lower number) plug and vice versa. You should have a range of plugs available.

In-flight mixture control

Some manufacturers offer the option of an adjustable control IFM carburettor which allows the main needle valve to be adjusted from the transmitter. While is not essential, it does enable the pilot to alter the needle valve setting during flight. It is worth bearing the option in mind as a possible future requirement when choosing a transmitter or looking at the carburettor options available on various engines.

Propellers

Perhaps the most important consideration must be the choice of propeller, since the purpose of the engine is to turn one. See what the manufacturer recommends as the optimum size but experiment with similar sizes. Currently, the pumped motors are turning 12×9 to 12×11 propellers. You may also find

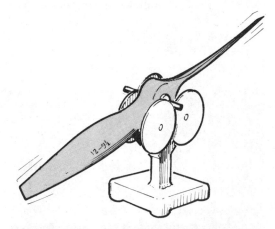

Ensure that the propeller is properly balanced. Either lightly sand the heavier blade, or brush on fuel proofer (or similar) to the lighter blade.

that different airframes with the same motor do not necessarily perform as well with the same propeller...

Tuned pipes

The more powerful motors are fitted with tuned pipes which give increased RPM, efficiency and reliability. To set them properly is a trial and error process, and a higher RPM will require a shorter pipe length for any given engine. RPM can, for example, be enhanced by increasing the percentage of nitro and/ or decreasing the diameter and/or pitch of the propeller.

Start with the manifold set at its longest length and shorten it by increments of a quarter of an inch until the desired *performance* is achieved. With aerobatic models, the pipe must be tuned to give maximum performance when climbing vertically rather than for best horizontal performance. For trial purposes, a supply of different lengths of spacers in silicone tube, starting at half an inch and going up in increments of a quarter of an inch, is invaluable. Pipe length is measured from the plug to the pipe's maximum thickness.

Setting up the engine for optimum performance

A tachometer is very useful when setting up the optimum combination of propeller, plug, pipe length and fuel. Be careful that you do not spend too much time in running up the engine on the ground, as it will rapidly overheat. Bear in mind also that the propeller will turn faster in the air. Taching the engine before every flight can also give an early warning of possible deterioration of the bearings before you can hear that they have failed. Keep records of your experiments in the following format:

ENGINE	NITRO	PROP	PIPE	PIPE LENGTH	WEATHER	REVS
ENYA (2) 60 XLF 4 GP	10%	12/9.5	OS	16.25 INS.	60 F WET	11,500

make notes here of how the model performed in flight

ENGINE	NITRO	PROP	PIPE	PIPE LENGTH	WEATHER	REVS
ENYA (2) 60 XLF 4 GP	15%	12/9.5	OS	16 INS	60 F WET	11,600

notes of the performance in flight

ENYA, YS and OS pumped motors. (Photos: P. Chinn & Tim Allison)

If you have a noise meter, add a column for that reading. The rules are that the noise should be less than 98 db at three metres.

So, which engine?

There is no one right answer, and brand loyalty and availability may well affect your choice. The current (1990) British team use different engines, ENYA, OS and YS, all of which are pumped. However here is a checklist of some points to take into consideration

—The engine should be easy to start, run consistently throughout the flight and respond evenly to throttle changes, be they gradual or sudden;
—Check what other modellers are using in the same or similar model and observe its performance;
—Go for slightly more power than recommended, have regard, but a healthy one, for bhp output as claimed by the manufacturer. If your budget allows for it, opt for a pumped motor;
—Select an engine which, all other things being equal, has an arrangement which makes bearing changes easy to do;
—Consider the availability of in-flight mix as a possible future requirement.

Laying up

After the last flight of the day, run the engine dry and then lay it up by injecting a liberal dosing of oil. This should help reduce any corrosive effect of the fuel. Before the first run of the day, flush the lay-up oil out with fuel.

Chapter 4
Choosing a radio

MOST OF YOU will already have radio gear and are probably loyal to the brand you use. The real question is not so much which brand but what characteristics should you be looking for, perhaps in the longer term? There is no reason why any of the good quality basic sets from any of the leading manufacturers should not be used.

FM or PCM?

The choice of FM or PCM is a matter of personal preference but remember that it is the PCM receivers which offer a failsafe facility. When interference occurs, the receiver will hold its last good command for one second and then go into failsafe which can either hold all servos as at the last good command or set them in a preprogrammed position. The model will fly through small patches of interference without a twitch or bump. When setting failsafe, remember

that you will not know which attitude the model will be in when interference occurs. It is generally best to set the model to hold all functions and shut the throttle to tick over. There is very little point, for example, in setting the failsafe to put the model into a gentle turn if, when interference occurs, the model is, say, inverted or in a vertical dive. Another point to consider is the lowering of the undercarriage, if fitted, as a visual sign that failure has occurred.

Computerised sets

Computerised sets are now available and, although they are more expensive, it may be worth spending a little time on considering what they have to offer. For the serious aerobatic flier, they are essential in the longer term and, if you are contemplating buying another transmitter, think very seriously about a computerised one. They can be used as

●T9VAP TRANSMITTER CONTROLS

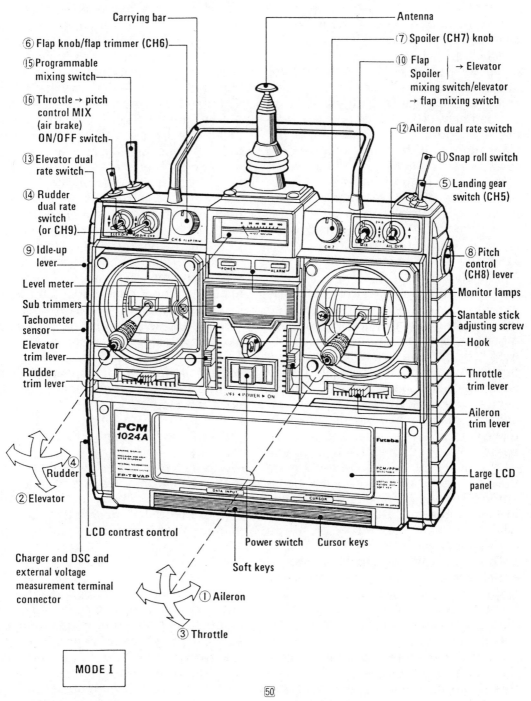

Carrying bar

Antenna

⑥ Flap knob/flap trimmer (CH6)

⑦ Spoiler (CH7) knob

⑮ Programmable mixing switch

⑩ Flap Spoiler } → Elevator mixing switch/elevator → flap mixing switch

⑯ Throttle → pitch control MIX (air brake) ON/OFF switch

⑫ Aileron dual rate switch

⑬ Elevator dual rate switch

⑪ Snap roll switch

⑭ Rudder dual rate switch (or CH9)

⑤ Landing gear switch (CH5)

⑨ Idle-up lever

⑧ Pitch control (CH8) lever

Level meter

Monitor lamps

Sub trimmers

Slantable stick adjusting screw

Tachometer sensor

Hook

Elevator trim lever

Throttle trim lever

Rudder trim lever

Aileron trim lever

④ Rudder

Large LCD panel

② Elevator

LCD contrast control

Power switch   Cursor keys

Charger and DSC and external voltage measurement terminal connector

Soft keys

① Aileron

③ Throttle

MODE I

50

Futaba 1024A PCM transmitter
(*courtesy Ripmax/Futaba*)

21

basic sets to begin with, by programming out or inhibiting the features which are not required. They can then be introduced one by one as needs, demand and experience increases.

Look at a typical top-of-the-range computer set. It comes with receiver and servos in an aluminium protective case and has the capability of storing the settings for several models, so you are really getting the equivalent of six transmitters. It has the usual servo reverse, rates and trimmer functions. It also has a built-in tachometer, audible battery-low alarm, a timer with an audible alarm which can be set to count either up or down and, of course, failsafe. Computer sets offer other functions and features which are invaluable.

Probably the first thing to be noticed is that the servos only need to be installed with rough alignment and without too much concern about the size of the output arms, orientation of the servo throw or centring the control surface through the linkage to the arm onto the centre of the servo head. Mechanical adjustments are a thing of the past. Gone are the days when clevises had to be unhooked and unscrewed two and a half turns, or the position of the arm on the servo head rotated an extra notch anti-clockwise, or additional holes drilled in the servo arms, etc. The electronics will take care of most of these adjustments.

The amount of travel of the servo arm either side of neutral is adjusted by the **Adjustable Travel Volume** (ATV). This function allows you to program in differential movement. For example, the elevator usually requires more down than up throw to overcome the effect of the incidence of the wing. ATV allows this differential to be programmed in and helps make the elevator response 'feel' the same for inside and outside manoeuvres.

The **Adjustable Function Rate** (AFR) can be useful if separate servos are used for the ailerons, each controlled by different channels but mixed together by the program. To alter the amount of surface movement the ATVs for each channel would normally need to be adjusted but the AFR allows the 'mixed' throw to be increased or decreased.

The **Trim** function allows the amount of servo travel per click of the trim lever to be increased or decreased.

Mixing. There are various mixing facilities available whereby two or more channels are 'mixed' together so that they operate from a single switch or lever, for example master/slave mixing. Consider flying knife edge. In order to eliminate the pitching and rolling effects in some models when rudder is applied, the necessary correcting elevator/aileron movement can be mixed in by selecting rudder as master and elevator and ailerons as slaves. Thus, when rudder is applied, the correct amount of compensating elevator and aileron is automatically mixed in enabling accurate knife edge flight to be maintained.

Both **Dual Rates** and **Exponential** are included.

It is not possible to describe all the features the computer sets have to offer in an introductory book such as this, and a more detailed description can be gained by visiting a good model shop.

Servos

The choice of servos is governed by the amount of space for installation (for example the space for aileron servos in the wings), cost and performance. Servos in aerobatic models are in *continuous* use throughout each flight and the loads placed upon them are considerable.

Chapter 5
Trimming the model

TRIMMING is a *very* critical stage in the preparation of the model for aerobatic flying. It is a painstaking and time-consuming exercise which may require many flights before the model is properly trimmed. However, if it is skimped the model may never be capable of flying accurate aerobatic manoeuvres, however competent the pilot. Each aspect has to be taken in turn, and then revisited as other adjustments are made, until the model flies satisfactorily. It is useful, if not essential, to keep a record of what has been done, so get an assistant to write down your comments during each flight and then note what action was taken to attempt to correct any fault.

There are several aspects to trimming. It all began at the building stage when care was taken to make sure the model was built true and the engine aligned with the amount of side and downthrust as per the instructions. Any tolerable amount of warp in the wings was lost at the centre. The wings were measured, balanced and then aligned at the stated angle of incidence. Having built the model true and checked it for the correct C of G and lateral balance on the ground, the time has come to trim it in the air.

Be prepared to make temporary adjustments at the flying site. Have packing and washers at the ready in case down and sidethrust need to be altered. Blu-tac or Plasticine are useful for adding weight temporarily to the wings and front or rear of the fuselage to adjust lateral balance or C of G. Temporary adjustments can be made permanent later at home. The overall objective in trimming is to set the model up in such a way that it can perform accurate aerobatics.

What is involved?

There is no preset order for the trimming sequence as the resultant change from one exercise may well require a previous trimming flight to be reflown. The sequence followed in this chapter is a useful guide, but if the prevailing conditions prevent you from carrying out one of the trimming manoeuvres properly, leave it until another day and continue with the next.

Trimming starts with checking the dihedral of the wings. This is followed by aligning the engine and setting the C of G and lateral balance of the model. The next stage is to achieve a state whereby each control surface is seen to act independently and without introducing extraneous changes in direction as if another control surface had been applied. Finally, the settings of throws, rates and similar functions can be fine-tuned to suit your style of flying.

A properly trimmed model should fly straight and true when upright or inverted (with a little down elevator to overcome the effect of the positive incidence of the wing), fly on knife edge without climbing/diving or pulling to-wards or away from the canopy, roll axially and loop without deviating to either side.

At best the trimming exercise will be a compromise and it may still be neces-sary to apply 'in-flight' trim and use control adjustments to compensate for the prevailing conditions on the day. It is also possible that you may not have flown some of the trimming manoeuvres correctly and, as your flying skills improve, it would be worth carrying out the trimming exercise again.

Needless to say, trimming is best carried out on a calm day or with only a slight wind.

Get used to the model first

Start by setting the throws in accordance with the instructions supplied with the model and ensure that all surfaces move freely. Always be on the alert for any sign of stress on the servos at the extremities of stick movements by listening for the buzzing sound of a stalled servo. The control surfaces must centre accurately when the sticks are returned to the neutral position.

Use the first few flights to become familiar with the model. Try flying gentle loops, rolls and inverted until you feel comfortable with the settings of the throws and the 'feel' of the model. It may be necessary to alter the control throws to suit your personal preference to eliminate any 'twitchiness' and to make sure the amount of response seems reasonable before you start to trim the model in earnest.

All trimming passes should be made at a distance and altitude that will enable you to make an accurate assessment of any deviations that occur. There will be some occasions when the model is best observed viewed from the side, and others in plan view.

Dihedral angle

Imagine your high wing trainer. When rudder is applied the model yaws, one wing lifts, the other drops and a banking turn is initiated. If the dihedral angle was gradually reduced the ideal situation would be reached (probably anhedral with a high wing) when the rudder would produce no sign of rolling, but yaw the model with possibly some pitching as if up or down elevator has been applied. If the dihedral angle was reduced further still, the application of rudder would cause roll in the opposite direction.

The test for correct dihedral is best carried out with the model in knife edge flight, first rolled to the left so that the rudder stick needs to be moved to the *right* to keep the nose of the model up, ie.

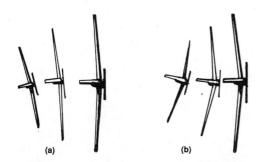

Checking dihedral. Model is on right rudder (to keep the nose up). (a) Model is rolling against rudder—increase dihedral; (b) Model is rolling with rudder—reduce dihedral.

on *right rudder*, and then on *left rudder*.

Fly the model away from you on full throttle and roll it onto knife edge and adjust the rudder to maintain level flight. Watch the model carefully.

If it tends to roll with rudder—reduce dihedral.
If it tends to roll against rudder—increase dihedral.

The only way to correct the dihedral angle is to reset the wings. With foam wings it is a matter of peeling back the covering and sawing through the top skin. The dihedral angle can be altered by adding slivers of plywood or slicing away the foam as required, and gluing them back together. Alter the dihedral in increments of a quarter of an inch and make sure wing halves are properly aligned and reinforced at the centre.

You will know the dihedral is correct when the model flies for ten seconds and more on knife edge, using only rudder and elevator to maintain altitude and heading, before any rolling becomes apparent.

This 'rolling with rudder' is one of the few faults that can be guaranteed to be corrected eventually.

Throttle

Check that the throttle moves freely from fully closed, trim shut, to fully open. Not all carburettors have a linear response and a half throttle setting on the control stick may not be a true half throttle setting on the motor. Differentials may be required to compensate for this. A tachometer is useful in that you will be able to ascertain maximum revs and then note the position where the quarter, half, and threequarter settings are on the stick. You need to be able to get a feel for the rate at which the stick should be moved to achieve smooth and even throttle response.

Sidethrust

The spiralling slipstream from the propeller hits the fin and rudder at an angle. This causes the model to weathercock as though it were in a crosswind and rudder trim is applied to bring it back on heading. Unfortunately the amount of trim required depends on the throttle setting, and whenever the throttle is altered the model will change its heading. The only way to trim the model to head straight at all throttle settings without having to continually feed in rudder corrections is to adjust the sidethrust.

Fly the model into wind and away from you at full throttle. With the rudder at *neutral* and the wings level pull up into a vertical climb. The model should climb straight and, after some distance (about four seconds), veer slightly to the left.

If the model veers right—decrease right thrust.
If the model veers too early to the left—increase right thrust.

Adjust the sidethrust so that the model flies straight with the rudder in

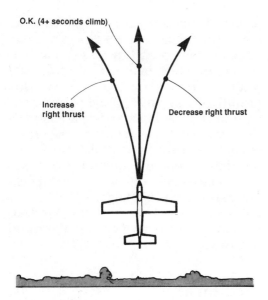

O.K. (4+ seconds climb)

Increase right thrust

Decrease right thrust

Checking side thrust.

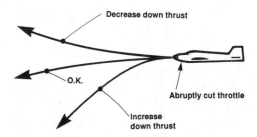

Decrease down thrust

O.K.

Abruptly cut throttle

Increase down thrust

Checking down thrust.

the neutral position thus avoiding the need for permanent trim to hold the model straight.

One to seven degrees of sidethrust may be needed depending on the design of the model.

Downthrust

A fully symmetrical wing produces equal lift on both sides. To ensure the wings produce lift they are aligned with a slightly positive angle of incidence. At any given throttle setting this may cause the model to climb or dive when it is flown straight and level unless elevator correction is applied. It is essential that aerobatic models fly straight and level with neutral elevator whatever the throttle setting and the way to do this is to introduce a little downthrust.

Fly the model upright and straight and level into wind and across in front of you at full throttle. The model will be in side view with the elevator at *neutral* and the wings level. Abruptly close the throttle, hold it closed for three seconds and then

open it up. The model should still be in level flight, or in a very slight dive.

If the model dives more than just gently—increase downthrust.
If the model climbs—decrease downthrust.

Adjust the downthrust so that the model maintains the same altitude with the elevator in the neutral position, thus avoiding the need for permanent trim to hold the model straight.

Up to three degrees of downthrust may be needed.

Centre of Gravity

A *slightly* rearward C of G is required in aerobatic models to reduce inherent stability and enable the control surfaces to act more responsively.

Fly the model across in front of you into wind with the throttle fully open at a height equivalent to the top line of the box. Fly the model straight and level, throttle back to tickover and push the model into a vertical dive and neutralise (hands off) the controls.

If the model pulls towards the cockpit, the C of G may be too far forward. Within the design limitations of the model a slightly more rearward C of G may correct this.

Try to adjust the C of G by repositioning items such as the battery pack in preference to adding weights. It is worth remembering that if the fuel tank is not mounted over the C of G, the C of G will change as fuel is used up.

Lateral or left/right balance, and wing warp

Although the static tests will have enabled you to sort out any nasties during the building stage this trimming exercise must be carried out to ensure the model performs looping manoeuvres without going off-track and that it can maintain level flight with the trims neutral. An out-of-balance wing will pull the model off-line in level and vertical flight or cause a wing to drop when the throttle is closed. It is sometimes very difficult to determine if the cause of a model going off-heading is through incorrect sidethrust, wing warp or an out-of-balance wing, or a combination of all three.

Fly the model into wind (preferably a slight breeze) and away from you upright and at full throttle with the wings *level*. Pull the model into a series of four of five loops using elevator only, ie. *no* rudder and *no* aileron movements. If the lateral balance is wrong or there is a warp in the wings the model will corkscrew in the direction of the lower, probably heavier, wing. Repeat this but with the model inverted, again using elevator only. If the model corkscrewed in the *opposite* direction, wing weights are needed. Add Plasticine to the lighter wing and repeat the tests until the model flies true.

After the flying session the Plasticine

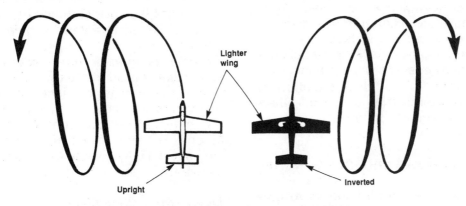

Model corkscrews in the opposite direction—add weight to the lighter wing.

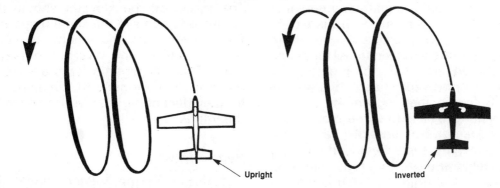

Model corkscrews in the same direction—warped wing.

can be weighed and the same amount of metal in the form of screws or nails can be concealed in the wingtip.

However, if the model corkscrewed in the *same* direction then a warp in the wings is having an effect. Ideally the wings should be cut and corrected or replaced. If the problem is slight and you think you can live with it, it may be possible to correct the problem by adding a trim tab to the underside of the down-going wing. Otherwise the ailerons will have to be adjusted to compensate for the warp. As it is impossible to achieve the two states of trim that are needed, one for level flight and the second for looping manoeuvres, a choice of which compromise solution has to be made. You have a choice of trimming the ailerons so that the model loops correctly and be prepared to fly out its tendency to roll in level flight. Alternatively you can trim the model so that it does not roll in level flight and accept the need to claw the model back on to line whenever a looping manoeuvre is performed. The ideal situation is when no aileron trim is needed whatever the speed of the model.

Setting throws and rate switches

The choice of setting controls to give either a 'twitchy' or 'soft' response to stick movement is a matter for personal choice. However most transmitters have rate switches, and the more advanced sets have additional functions which enable you to program in surface throws for snaps, rolls and so on. Before embarking on the road of attempting to build in as many aids from the transmitter as possible, remember that just flying the schedule in the right sequence and in the right place is demanding enough so avoid having to think of too many extra things to switch

on and off! Another problem is that you may program something in which is perfect for the flying conditions when you set it, but what happens when those conditions change? It is probably best to fly every manoeuvre by the sticks and use rates, etc., only when it is absolutely necessary. This approach will certainly help you become a more accomplished pilot.

Ailerons for rolling (roll)

The rate of roll should be in the region of three rolls in five seconds on full stick movement but there is no hard and fast rule. Flying styles do change over the years and you may decide to increase or decrease the roll rate to suit your own evolving style.

An aerobatic model must be trimmed so it rolls at the same rate in both directions. Take each direction of roll in turn and ask an assistant to help you with the timing.

To achieve an *axial* roll, ie. when the model rotates around the thrust line as though there was a piece of wire holding it rock steady on its longitudinal axis, may require differential on the ailerons. The movement of the down-going aileron may need to be reduced to achieve this.

Elevator for looping (pitch)

The throw on the elevator should be adjusted to achieve the same response for a given stick movement for both upright (inside) and inverted (outside) loops. This will normally require a larger downward movement to compensate for the effect of the positive incidence of the wings.

Rudder (yaw)

The throw on the rudder should be adjusted to achieve the same response in both directions for a given stick movement.

Faults which cannot be rectified

Trimming is, at best, a compromise and however much care is taken some faults may still remain. Possible examples have been discussed in this book, including warped wings and pitching and rolling in knife edge flight. It is for you to decide if you can live with such faults—many pilots do—but remember the computerised radios will enable some minor faults to be 'mixed out'.

As with the whole trimming process, as you alter one aspect another may be aggravated.

Trimming check list

1) Make sure you have sufficient tools, etc., to carry out temporary adjustments at the flying site.
2) Carry a notebook and pen to record progress.
3) Try and get someone to help.
4) Dihedral.
5) Throttle.
6) Sidethrust.
7) Downthrust.
8) Centre of Gravity.
9) Lateral balance and warps.
10) Aileron throws.
11) Elevator throws.
12) Rudder throws.
13) Mixing out.

Chapter 6
Flying the basic components

THERE ARE hundreds, if not thousands, of different aerobatic manoeuvres, all made up from a combination of five basic components—the line, the loop, the roll, the stall and the spin. It should follow, then, that having mastered these components it should be possible to fly any manoeuvre. Well, it is never quite that simple but the first step is to understand and to practise flying the basic components before trying complete manoeuvres.

There are two terms which need to be clarified—'Flightpath' and 'Attitude':

a) the flightpath of the model is the trajectory of its centre of gravity and it is upon *this* line that judging is based unless otherwise stated;
b) The attitude is the direction of the fuselage centreline in relation to the flightpath.

The drawing shows that, although the model is turned into wind, its flightpath is following a straight line and so the model is being flown correctly, even though its appearance is somewhat ungainly.

Now is also the time to start concentrating on flying within the limits of the aerobatic box.

Distance

Attempt to position all flights at a distance of 150 metres and get used to judging that distance in relation to the apparent size of the model. Ask a friend to pace out 150 metres and stand there during a flight. He can signal that the model is too close in by turning to face you, that it is too far out by turning his back towards you and that the model is at about the correct distance by turning his side towards you.

The box

There are three elements; the side

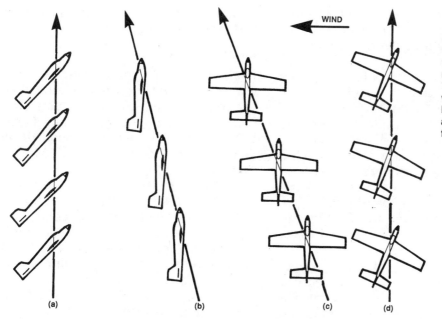

WIND

(a) and (d) Following the *correct* vertical flightpath; note the attitude of the model. (b) and (c) The model has a vertical attitude but fails to follow a vertical flightpath.

(a) (b) (c) (d)

limits, the Top Line and the Base Line.

The size of the box (see Chapter 1) is defined in terms of degrees. This can be measured by using a protractor or the span of the stretched hand held at arms length. The distance between the top of the thumb and little finger subtends an angle of just about fifteen degrees. Thus four spans either side of the centreline establishes the outer limits of the box.

It is normal at competitions for markers to be used to denote the centreline and outer limits of the box. At a local site it may be possible to use landmarks on the horizon or to place tall stakes into the ground to identify them.

Although it is not feasible to use a physical marker to show the top line, its height can be assessed as roughly four hand spans from the ground measured from a point 150 metres out.

The optimum height for the base line is difficult to define. Set too high and manoeuvres become squashed, too low and the model does not present itself well and can merge with trees or buildings on the horizon, and there is the danger that the model will not have

time to recover from an error situation. A low base line tends to exaggerate any difference between the entry and exit heights of a manoeuvre. Try one hand span (ie. 15 degrees) from the ground to start with.

The effect of the control surfaces

When learning the basic components think about the contribution each of the control surfaces can make. Although throttle, rudder, ailerons and elevator interact, their effect, in broad terms, requires the use of:

a) rudder, which causes yaw, to keep the correct distance and stay on that 150 metre line. If the wind is blowing in or out learn to use the rudder to steer the model back on line. In extreme situations it may be necessary to resort to using ailerons but avoid doing this in a high scoring manoeuvre. The terms *left* and *right* are used to denote the direction in which the stick on the transmitter should be moved.

31

b) ailerons, which cause roll, to keep the wings level otherwise the model will turn towards the dropping wing when elevator is applied. This can cause all sorts of problems such as taking the model way off the 150 metre line, delaying the start of the next component while the error is corrected, distorting the shape of the manoeuvre and so on. The terms *left* and *right* are used to denote the direction in which the stick on the transmitter should be moved.

c) elevator, which causes pitching, to maintain the flightpath at the correct angle for the manoeuvre. Horizontal flight must be parallel to the ground, vertical lines must be at 90 degrees to the ground and 45-degree lines at that precise angle. Loops must be pulled or pushed just sufficiently to ensure the exit line is at the correct angle. A tendency to under or overpull/push will ruin the shape of a manoeuvre. The terms *pull* and *push* are used to denote the direction in which the stick on the transmitter should be moved.

d) throttle, within the limits of the performance of the engine, to maintain a constant speed throughout the flight, apart from any stall manoeuvres, of course. Full throttle will be used for entry into vertical and rolling manoeuvres, while power should reduced when descending. Terms such as *idle, half* and *full* are used to denote the amount of throttle which *may* be required depending on the performance of your own set up.

The basic components

Learn to fly each component from left to right and right to left, upright and inverted and be able to compensate for all crosswind situations.

Any new manoeuvres should be learned at a relatively high altitude to allow plenty of time to recover if things go wrong.

Lines

Every manoeuvre starts and finishes with a horizontal line. Some manoeuvres in the current Standard Schedule include vertical and 45-degree lines. Lines at other angles will need to be learned for the Senior and Master Schedules.

Practise by devising a set of linked 'line' patterns. Horizontal lines should, subject to confidence and ability, be flown on the base line and the top limit of the box. Vertical lines should be flown on the centreline, the box limits and halfway between the box limits and centreline. They should be entered from upright and inverted horizontal flight and from the base line and the top of the box as appropriate. Forty-five degree lines should ascend and descend between the base line and the top limit of the box starting on the centreline and imaginary lines between the centreline and the box limits. Get used to thinking about *pushing* and *pulling* into the part loops.

A possible sequence is:

1) fly a rectangle with the model starting upright, the limits being the base line, top of the box and outer box limits. Try this from right to left, then left to right, and then repeat these with the model starting from inverted.

2) as for (1) but introduce a vertical line in the centre.

3) as for (2) but introduce vertical lines halfway between the centreline and outer box limits (five vertical lines in all).

4) As for (1) but introduce 45-degree lines between the base line and the top line. Start them from the centre in ascending and descending directions.

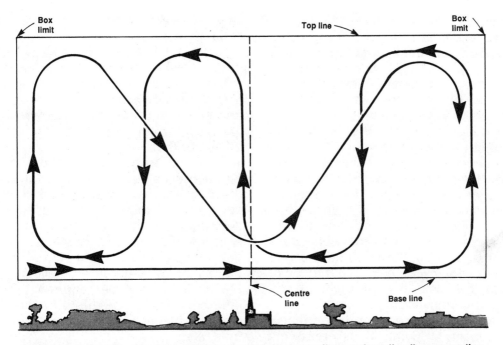

Possible training sequence for vertical, horizontal, 45-degree lines and small radius connecting part loops.

Do not worry too much about the accuracy of the corners but they will need to be quite tight.

Loops

Complete or part loops may range from anything between a full circle to an eighth of a circle, and must be flown entirely in the vertical plane.

A loop must have a constant radius and, if a manoeuvre consists of part

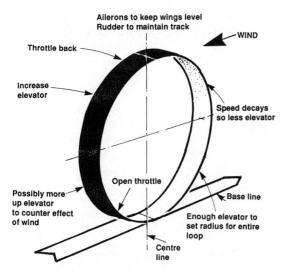

Using controls to maintain symmetry in an inside loop.

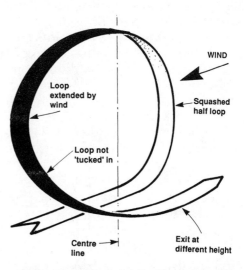

A 'distorted' loop through failure to use elevator correctly to adjust for the effect of the wind, and possibly through trying to fly too large a manoeuvre for the performance of the model.

loops connected with lines, the radii of those part loops must be constant.

Again the points to watch for reflect the pilot's ability to use the rudder to keep the right distance, the elevator/throttle for constant radius and the ailerons to keep the wings level.

Practise by flying the sequences devised for the 'lines' but concentrate on the correct flying of the part loops which join the various lines together. Then try flying complete loops starting from and finishing on the centreline. These should start and finish with horizontal lines. Try the full loops starting first from the base line and then from the top of the box. Again try all of these from left to right, right to left, upright and inverted.

It may help to understand the effect of the rudder by flying loops crosswind either towards you or away from you on the 'B' axis and note the extent to which the use of rudder helps to keep the model on line.

Rolls

A roll is the rotation of the model around its longitudinal axis. It may be a full 360 degrees or any part of that and be continuous, or hesitated on points such as in a four-point roll when the model performs four 90-degree rolls in the same direction, each separated by an equal time interval. The rate of roll may range from less than a second to several seconds depending on the manoeuvre.

The rate of roll must be constant, there must be a crisp, well-defined start and finish and, if the roll is flown on a line between part loops, it must be in the middle of that line.

Slow rolls are quite difficult to master. Before practising the slow roll, consider the interaction of the various control surfaces and therefore the position of the sticks as the roll is flown. The ailerons will rotate the model at a rate depending on the amount of movement but, as the roll progresses, elevator and rudder input will be required during different parts of the roll to maintain a constant height. The throttle will be kept fully open.

Fly a four-point hesitation roll, ie. a series of quarter rolls, holding the hesitations for as long as necessary to get used to the position of the sticks. Then gradually reduce the length of the hesitations until a continuous roll is achieved.

Practise flying full and half-rolls in the middle of the lines of your devised schedule. Try rolling to the right and the left. Practise flying slow rolls along the bottom line in both directions.

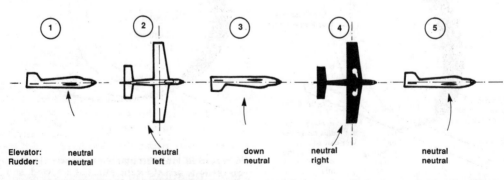

Elevator:	neutral	neutral	down	neutral	neutral
Rudder:	neutral	left	neutral	right	neutral

Consider a slow roll to the *right*. Initially this is best flown away from you so that you can observe the effect of rudder and elevator at the various points of roll.

Stall turn

The essence of a stall is that the speed of the model is reduced until the model cannot remain airborne, the controls have little or no effect and it falls towards the ground. In the stall turn, the stall is executed when the model is tracking a vertical up line and rudder is applied just before the point of stall so the model pivots around the longitudinal axis and tracks a downward path. In a crosswind stall turns are normally made towards the wind.

Opposite rudder may need to be applied, as though it were a brake, just before a vertical down line is reached, in order to hold the model on the down line and then to prevent the model swinging like a pendulum. Rudder corrections with corresponding elevator corrections (to prevent pitching) may also need to be applied to keep the model on a straight flightpath. The maximum allowable radius for the pivot is half a wingspan. The yawing action over the stall may need to be assisted by a blip of throttle. Elevator is used to maintain the vertical attitude of the model. The throttle should be opened to overcome the stalled attitude of the model and elevator should be used with great care until flying speed has been obtained otherwise the model may stall and drop a wing into a spin on exit.

Practise flying stall turns at either end of the box, entering upright and inverted. Try also executing a half-roll in either the up or down line, or both, to reinforce the learning of the direction of the application of the rudder and elevator.

Spin

Spins may be either positive (upright) or negative (inverted). A positive spin requires up elevator, the ailerons to be applied in the direction of the spin and rudder applied in the same direction as the spin. A negative spin requires down elevator, the ailerons to be applied in the direction of the spin and rudder applied in the opposite direction to the spin.

To execute a positive spin the model tracks a horizontal flightpath into wind on the top line. The engine speed is slowly reduced to idle while, at the same time, the elevator is gradually increased to keep the nose up until the model stalls. At the stall the model will normally drop its nose and one wing and the spin should follow the dropping wing. Aileron, rudder and elevator should be applied to keep the model on a downward vertical line.

Exit from the spin into a vertical line down is achieved by neutralising (letting go of) the sticks up to half a turn before the desired attitude for the model is reached.

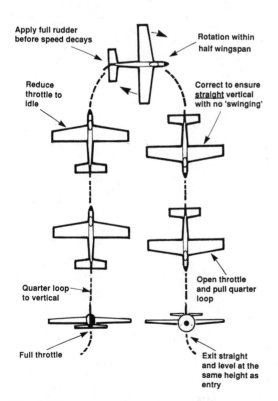

Apply full rudder before speed decays

Rotation within half wingspan

Reduce throttle to idle

Correct to ensure <u>straight</u> vertical with no 'swinging'

Quarter loop to vertical

Open throttle and pull quarter loop

Full throttle

Exit straight and level at the same height as entry

The stall turn.

In a correctly executed stalled spin, the model will spin slowly and may seem jerky. If the entry speed was too fast the model will snap roll (climb on entry) into the spin.

Practise by flying along the top line and timing the stall and spin to track down the centreline. Try this in both directions.

Finally, do not spend an inordinate amount of time just practising the basic components otherwise boredom may set in. After half a dozen flights or so try some of the manoeuvres in the schedule.

Chapter 7
Flying the Standard Schedule

THIS CHAPTER analyses the component parts of each manoeuvre in the current (1990) Standard Schedule, gives hints on how they should be flown, suggests calls which the caller may make and lists possible downgrades.

A constant wind direction can never be guaranteed, even on the same day, and it is important to learn to fly the schedule starting into wind from right to left *and* from left to right. You should also learn to cope with all the possible crosswind situations (ie. with a crosswind blowing 'in' or 'out') so four basic ways of flying the schedule need to be learned.

All manoeuvres start and finish in straight and level flight. Centre manoeuvres start and finish on the same heading and turnround manoeuvres finish at a heading 180 degrees to entry.

The schedules are changed every few years but the principles of learning to fly

them do not. For ease of illustration this chapter assumes that the wind direction is blowing from the right and therefore that the first manoeuvre will be flown from *left* to *right*.

Armchair rehearsal

Before attempting the full Standard Schedule it is necessary to understand how each of the individual manoeuvres is made up and how they should, in theory, be flown. Start by flying them in 'the armchair', by 'walking' through the individual components that make up the manoeuvre and working through the action of the sticks and the possible effect of wind direction. It helps to use a small toy model and hand fly it through the manoeuvres noting the direction of travel required of the elevator, rudder, ailerons and throttle as each component is executed.

Size of manoeuvre

This will be limited by the performance of the model and possibly further affected by the strength and direction of the wind. Manoeuvres with half or larger loops such as Immelman Turns, Half (Reverse) Cuban Eights and Full Loops need to be flown with as large a radius as possible without there being much sign that the model is struggling when it reaches the top line. All such manoeuvres should be of a consistent size throughout the schedule.

Quarter loops are used to connect two lines (eg. as in a square loop) and so need to have a much smaller radius in order to ensure there is sufficient room for the other component parts of the manoeuvre.

Straight and level

Ailerons are used to keep the wings level at all times unless, of course, the model is rolled.

The rudder is used, except in knife edge flight, to keep the model on track at a constant distance. Confusion can sometimes arise when the model is inverted. Remember that, when the model is tracking a continuous line, the direction of the application of the rudder remains constant. For example when you fly an inside loop, the fact that the model is inverted at the top does not affect the direction of the application of rudder to keep the model, say, heading out. However if the model is flying a continuous line, at whatever angle, and is half rolled, then the rudder will act in the opposite sense and if, say, right rudder was needed to maintain the heading when the model was upright then left rudder will be needed when the model has half rolled.

Building up confidence

To begin with you will probably want to restrict each flight to the practice of just one or two manoeuvres, and gradually build up your repertoire until you can fly all the manoeuvres in the schedule. Before each flight be clear in your own mind what you are going to attempt and 'fly' each manoeuvre in your mind, talking yourself through the stick movements.

When you feel reasonably confident with flying the manoeuvres individually, try the complete schedule. If a mistake is made, ignore it and carry on to the next manoeuvre. Use the next flight to practise the faulty manoeuvre but lead up to it with the preceding manoeuvre or two as it may well be that it was the incorrect execution of, or wrong exit from, preceding manoeuvres which forced an error into one that is normally flown perfectly well on its own!

The role of the caller

Your caller/helper will normally assist with the preparation of the model for flight and retrieve it after the completion of the schedule. During the flight he is allowed to stand behind the pilot and 'call'. It is up to the pilot to decide what he wants his caller to contribute and it can be very off-putting if the caller changes from the routine. Typically the caller will give advance confirmation of the next manoeuvre. He may also be required to help with positioning the model within the box by counting the model down to the centre line on central manoeuvres and warning the pilot of the likelihood of going outside the limits of the box. During the flight the pilot will have more than enough to concentrate on with flying the model and coping with the wind direction, and any 'calling' that is done must be kept brief and be said in time for the pilot to absorb it and be able to react to it.

The Standard Schedule for 1990 is:

No.	Manoeuvre	K Factor
1	Three Inside Loops	2
2	Stall Turn	2
3	Straight Inverted	2
4	½ Cuban Eight	1
5	Square Loop	2
6	Immelman Turn	1
7	Three Outside Loops (from the top)	3
8	½ Roll ½ Square Loop	1
9	Double Immelman	2
10	½ Reverse Cuban Eight	1
11	Slow Roll	3
12	½ Square Loop ½ Roll up	1
13	Three Turn Spin	2
		23

Score 125 points in two competitions to qualify for the Senior Class.

Judges award marks out of 10 for each individual manoeuvre.

The K Factor is the degree of difficulty attributed to a manoeuvre and the judges' mark is multiplied by that number. Thus a mark of 6 for an Immelman Turn would score 6 on the scoresheet but the same mark for a Slow Roll would score 18.

WIND

Finish

39

Take-off and landing

Take-off and landing sequences are not specified as part of the Standard Schedule. However they are described and it is worth including them as part of the schedule even though they do not attract any marks.

The take-off sequence (optional sequence)

Description

1. The model is placed on the runway and takes off;
2. The model turns 90 degrees towards the upwind marker;
3. When approximately over the marker the model turns 270 degrees for a downwind trimming pass;
4. When approximately level with the downwind marker the model initiates a 180-degree turn *or* a reversal manoeuvre of the pilot's choice to place the model at the *correct distance* and on the chosen *base line*;
5. The model is steadied in readiness for entry into the first manoeuvre.

This sequence, when marked, attracts either *zero* or *ten* points.

Downgrade

Model does not follow the take-off sequence—*zero* points

The landing sequence (optional sequence)

Description

1. On completion of the final maneuvre, at reduced power the model executes a 180-degree turn to a downwind heading;
2. Fly a downwind leg;

3. The model turns 180 degrees into wind for a landing approach.
4. The model touches down within the landing zone (as defined by the Competition Director);
5. The landing sequence is complete when the model has rolled ten yards.

This manoeuvre, when marked, attracts either *zero* or *ten* points.

Downgrades

Model does not follow the landing sequence—*zero points*
   If any undercarriage leg retracts on landing—*zero* points
   Model lands outside the landing zone—*zero* points

Three inside loops

Description

The model pulls up and executes three consecutive inside loops. All loops must be round and superimposed.

Caller's contribution

a) Remind the pilot the manoeuvre is three inside loops.
b) As this is the first manoeuvre in the schedule, tell the judge that the schedule is commencing but *only when the pilot says to do so.*
c) Count the model down, eg. *3—2—1—centre*, to the centreline so the pilot can prepare to pull the loop exactly on the centreline.
d) Thereafter call *centre* when the model reaches the centreline on the top and bottom of the ensuing loops—leave it to the pilot to count the number of loops performed.

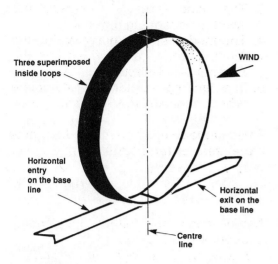

Three superimposed
inside loops

WIND

Horizontal
entry
on the base
line

Horizontal
exit on the
base line

Centre
line

Three inside loops.

e) Call next manoeuvre is *stall turn.*

Component parts

1. Horizontal Entry Line (on the *base line*).
2. Three Inside Loops.
3. Horizontal Exit Line (on the *base line*).

Clearly fix the size of the manoeuvre in your mind's eye before commencing it.

The model is flown at full throttle along the base line into wind; keep the wings level and adjust the track with rudder. Listen for the caller's countdown to the centreline and on 'centre' smoothly apply up elevator.

The first quarter of the loop sets the radius for the entire manoeuvre so

remember, less elevator is required in stronger winds. During the second quarter, to adjust for decaying speed and/or the effect of the wind, a reduction in elevator may be required. As the model flies inverted over the top of the loop, reduce the throttle and maintain the shape of the circle by increasing the' elevator. In the last quarter of the loop as the speed increases, more elevator may be required to ensure the model finishes the loop on the centreline and at the same height as the entry.

Concentration is needed to ensure the second and third loops are superimposed over the first and the call of 'centre' as the model passes the centreline should help you gauge the position.

Throughout the manoeuvre ailerons will be used to keep the wings level and rudder used to keep the model on the correct track.

Downgrades

ENTRY AND EXIT LINES:
flightpath not horizontal
absence of entry/exit lines
heading change
wings not level
entry and exit lines at different heights

LOOPS:
loops not round
loops not superimposed
heading change during loops
wings not level during loops
loops not centred on the centreline

Stall turn

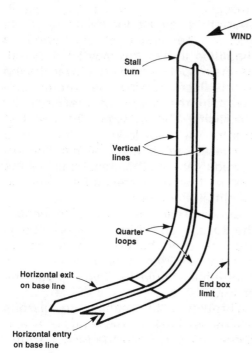

Stall turn.

Description

The model pulls up into a vertical attitude, executes a 180-degree stall turn in either direction, then recovers in level flight.

Caller's contribution

a) Give warning if the end box limit is likely to be exceeded;

b) Call next manoeuvre is *straight inverted flight*.

Component parts

1. Horizontal Entry Line (on the *base line*).
2. Quarter Inside Loop to Vertical Line Up.
3. Vertical Line Up.
4. Stall Turn.
5. Vertical Line Down.
6. Quarter Inside Loop to Horizontal.
7. Horizontal Exit Line (on the *base line*).

The model is flown at full throttle within the limit of the box and elevator is smoothly applied to form a quarter-loop into a vertical climb. Use the rudder, elevator and ailerons to keep the model tracking a vertical flightpath. Before the model reaches the top line and while it still has forward speed, reduce the throttle and just before all forward speed is lost apply rudder in the direction you wish it to turn. It may help to blip the throttle, thereby increasing the airflow over the surfaces to improve the response of the rudder. The vertical descent should be parallel and the same length to the up line and the radii of the quarter-loop exit onto the base line should match the first quarter-loop. The throttle should be opened to full before the model enters the horizontal exit line.

Throughout the manoeuvre, ailerons will be used to keep the wings level and rudder and elevator used to keep the model on the correct track.

Downgrades

ENTRY AND EXIT LINES:
flightpath not horizontal
absence of entry/exit lines
heading change
wings not level
entry and exit lines at different heights

QUARTER-LOOPS:
radii not constant
loops not round
heading change
wings not level

VERTICALS
flightpath not vertical
heading change
wings not level
absence of vertical lines
model oscillates on downward path

S<small>TALL</small>

radius of pivot exceeds half a wingspan

model flops towards/away from the pilot

Straight inverted flight

Description

The model half-rolls to inverted and flies straight and level inverted for a minimum of four seconds, then half-rolls back to level flight. The half-rolls may be in either direction.

Caller's contribution

a) Call *centre* as the model arrives at the centreline (this should allow the pilot to judge an equal distance of inverted flight either side of the centreline).
b) Call next manoeuvre is ½ *cuban eight*

Component parts

1. Horizontal Entry Line (on the *base line*).
2. Half-Roll to Inverted.
3. Horizontal Line Inverted.
4. Half-Roll to Upright.
5. Horizontal Exit Line (on the *base line*).

The model is flown at full throttle downwind and half-rolled to inverted at a point approximately midway between the box limit and the centreline. Some down elevator will be required to perform level inverted flight. Remember that the model is inverted and if track adjustments are necessary the rudder will act in the opposite sense. The call of 'centre' should help you gauge an equal distance on the other side of the centreline at which the model should be half-rolled to upright.

Throughout the manoeuvre ailerons will be used to keep the wings level and rudder used to keep the model on the correct track.

Downgrades

E<small>NTRY AND EXIT LINES:</small>

flightpath not horizontal

absence of entry/exit lines

heading change

wings not level

entry and exit lines at different heights

H<small>ALF-ROLLS:</small>

half-rolls not axial

heading change

roll rates not consistent

under or over-rolled

S<small>TRAIGHT AND LEVEL INVERTED FLIGHT:</small>

flightpath not horizontal

heading change

wings not level

flightpath not horizontal

inverted flight less than four seconds

manoeuvre not central to the centreline

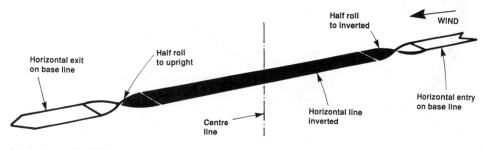

Straight inverted flight.

Half cuban eight

Description

The model pulls up and commences an inside loop, when at 45 degrees inverted the model does a half-roll then pulls up to recover in level flight.

Caller's contribution

a) Give warning if the end box limit is likely to be exceeded.
b) Call next manoeuvre *square inside loop*.

Component parts

1. Horizontal Entry Line (on the *base line*).
2. Five-eighths of an Inside Loop to a 45-Degree Downline Inverted.
3. Short 45-Degree Downline Inverted.
4. Half-Roll on 45-Degree Downline to Upright.
5. Short 45-Degree Line Down.
6. Eighth of an Inside Loop to Horizontal.
7. Horizontal Exit Line (on the *base line*).

The model is flown at full throttle towards the downwind box limit and using the elevator the model is smoothly pulled into a loop of similar size to that used in the first manoeuvre. The model is flown over the top of the loop to exit inverted on a 45-degree downward line. The throttle is reduced as the model flies a short straight line, is half-rolled to upright, flies another short straight line of the same length and, during the eighth loop exit onto the base line, the throttle is opened to full.

Throughout the manoeuvre the ailerons will be used to keep the wings level and rudder used to keep the model on the correct track. The elevator will be used smoothly to ensure the radius of the loop is constant.

Downgrades

ENTRY AND EXIT LINES:
flightpath not horizontal
absence of entry/exit lines
heading change
wings not level
entry and exit lines at different heights

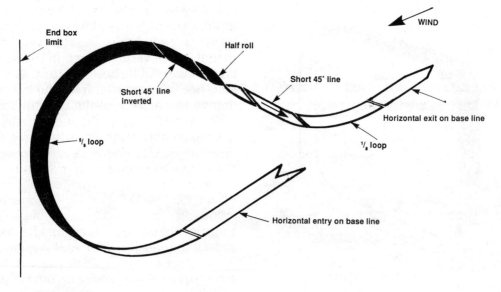

Half cuban eight.

LOOP SECTIONS:
radii not constant
loops not round
heading change
wings not level

SHORT 45-DEGREE LINES:
flightpath not at 45 degrees
heading change
wings not level
not of equal length

HALF-ROLL:
half-roll not axial
heading change
roll rate not consistent
under or over-roll

Square inside loop

Description

The model pulls up and performs an inside square loop.

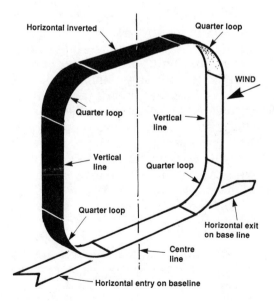

Square inside loop.

Caller's contributions

a) Calls *centre* as the model crosses the centreline.
b) Calls *centre* as the model crosses the top centreline.
c) Calls next manoeuvre *Immelman turn*.

Component parts

1. Horizontal Entry Line (on the *base line*).
2. Quarter Inside Loop to Vertical Line Up.
3. Vertical Line Up.
4. Quarter Inside Loop to Horizontal Inverted.
5. Horizontal Line Inverted.
6. Quarter Inside Loop to Vertical Line Down.
7. Vertical Line Down.
8. Quarter Inside Loop to Horizontal Upright.
9. Horizontal Exit Line (on the *base line*).

Clearly fix the size of the manoeuvre in your mind's eye before commencing it.

The model is flown at full throttle into wind. Listen for the call of 'centre', and after a short pause of, say, one to two seconds, smoothly quarter-loop the model into a vertical climb in the same way as you did for the stall turn. After a distance of twice that from the centre-line to the entry into the quarter-loop, pull a quarter-loop of the same radius so the model flies a horizontal line inverted downwind. Use down elevator to keep the model horizontal. Listen for the call of 'centre' to help you judge the length of this top line before pulling a quarter-loop into a vertical downline. The throttle should be eased to idle as it enters the vertical line. Pull a quarter-loop to exit at the same height and direction as entry, and open the throttle to full.

Throughout the manoeuvre ailerons will be used to keep the wings level and rudder and elevator used to keep the model on the correct track.

Downgrades

ENTRY AND EXIT LINES:
flightpath not horizontal
absence of entry/exit lines
heading change
wings not level

HORIZONTAL/VERTICAL LINES:
flightpath not horizontal/vertical
heading change
wings not level
lines of different lengths
horizontal lines not central

QUARTER-LOOPS:
radii not constant
loops not round
heading change
wings not level

GENERAL:
loop not square

Immelman turn

Description

The model pulls up and completes a half inside loop then *immediately* half-rolls to recover in level flight at a higher altitude than entry.

Caller's contribution

a) Give warning if the end box limits are likely to be exceeded.
b) Call next manoeuvre *three outside loops*.

Component parts

1. Horizontal Entry Line (on the *base line*).

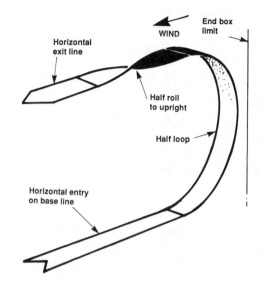

Immelman turn.

2. Half Inside Loop to Top Line Inverted.
3. Half-Roll to Upright.
4. Horizontal Exit Line (on the *top line*).

The size of the half-loop should be the same as that of the first manoeuvre. The danger lies in making the half-loop too small leaving insufficient height to fly the next manoeuvre!

The model is flown at full throttle within the limit of the box and up elevator is smoothly applied. The first quarter of the half-loop sets the radius for the manoeuvre so remember less elevator may be required in stronger winds. During the second quarter, to adjust for decaying speed and/or the effect of the wind, a reduction in elevator may be required. At the top of the loop the model is held inverted along a horizontal line and almost *immediately* half-rolled to upright.

Throughout the manoeuvre ailerons will be used to keep the wings level and rudder used to keep the model on the correct track.

Downgrades

ENTRY AND EXIT LINES:
flightpath not horizontal
absence of entry/exit lines
heading change
wings not level

HALF-LOOP:
radius not constant
loop not round
heading change
wings not level

HALF-ROLL:
half-roll not axial
heading change
roll rate not consistent
half-roll does not follow *immediately*
    after the half-loop
under or over-rolled

Three outside loops

Description

The model pushes over and executes three consecutive outside loops. All loops should be round and superimposed.

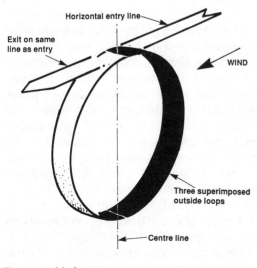

Horizontal entry line

Exit on same line as entry

WIND

Three superimposed outside loops

Centre line

Three outside loops.

Caller's contribution

a) Count the model down, eg. *3—2—1 —centre*, to the centreline so the pilot can prepare to push into the loop exactly on the centreline.
b) Thereafter calls *centre* as the model passes the centreline at the bottom and top of the ensuing loops.
c) Call next manoeuvre is *half-roll into half square loop.*

Component parts

1. Horizontal Entry Line (on the *top line*).
2. Three Outside Loops.
3. Horizontal Exit Line (on the *top line*).

Clearly fix the size of the manoeuvre in your mind's eye before commencing it. It should be similar to that of the first manoeuvre.

The model is flown at full throttle along the top line downwind. Keep the wings level and listen for the caller's countdown to the centre and on 'centre' reduce throttle and smoothly apply down elevator. As this manoeuvre is entered downwind, enough elevator needs to be applied to achieve the correct shape during the first quarter of the loop. During the second quarter of the loop, as speed increases, more down elevator may be required to maintain its shape and ensure the bottom of the loop is on the base line and at the centreline. Open the throttle to full just before the model passes the centreline inverted. The third quarter may require less elevator as the model is now flying into wind and this may need to be decreased further in the final quarter to adjust for decaying speed and/or the effect of the wind.

Concentration is needed to ensure the second and third loops are superimposed over the first and the call of 'centre' as the model passes the centreline should help gauge the model's position. Try and remember the point in the sky at which you entered the first loop as it is important to make sure the model climbs to just that height in the subsequent loops.

Throughout the manoeuvre ailerons will be used to keep the wings level and rudder used to keep the model on track.

Downgrades

ENTRY AND EXIT LINES:
entry and exit lines at different heights
flightpath not horizontal
absence of entry/exit lines
heading change
wings not level

LOOPS:
loops not round
loops not superimposed
heading changes during loops
wings not level during loops
loops not centred on the centreline

Half-roll into half square loop

Description

The model half-rolls to inverted then executes half of a square loop to recover in level flight at a lower altitude than entry.

Caller's contribution

a) Give warning if the end box limits are likely to be exceeded.
b) Call next manoeuvre *double Immelman*.

Component parts

1. Horizontal Entry Line (on the *top line*.

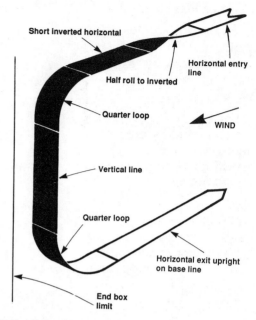

Half-roll into square loop.

2. Half-Roll to Inverted.
3. Short Horizontal Line Inverted.
4. Quarter Inside Loop to Vertical Line Down.
5. Vertical Line Down.
6. Quarter Inside Loop to Horizontal Line.
7. Horizontal Exit Line (on the *base line*).

The model is flown at full throttle downwind along the top line, and well within the limit of the box the model is half-rolled to inverted. After a short horizontal line with a little down elevator to keep the model level, the throttle is eased back and up elevator smoothly applied to form a quarter-loop into a vertical descent. Care now needs to be taken to time the smooth application of up elevator to form a quarter-loop of the same radius as the previous one so that the model exits upright along the base line.

Throughout the manoeuvre ailerons will be used to keep the wings level and rudder used to keep the model on the correct track.

Downgrades

Entry, short horizontal, vertical and exit lines:
flightpath not horizontal/vertical
absence of entry/exit lines
heading change
wings not level
short horizontal line not half the length
  of the down line

Half-roll:
half-roll not axial
heading change
roll rate not consistent
under or over-rolled

Quarter-loops:
radii not constant
loops not round
heading change
wings not level

General:
half-loop not square

Double Immelman

Description

The model pulls up into a half inside loop, half-rolls to upright, flies straight and level for approximately one second, does a half outside loop and half-rolls to level flight.

Caller's contribution

a) Call *centre* as the model crosses the centreline.
b) Call *centre* as the model crosses the top centreline.
c) Call next manoeuvre *half reverse cuban eight.*

Component parts

1. Horizontal Entry Line (on the *base line*).
2. Half Inside Loop to Inverted.
3. Half-Roll to Upright.
4. Horizontal Line.
5. Half Outside Loop to Inverted.
6. Half-Roll to Upright.
7. Horizontal Line continuing to Horizontal Exit Line (on the *base line*).

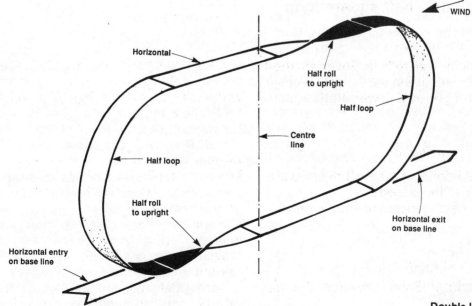

Double Immelman.

Clearly fix the size of the manoeuvre in your mind's eye before commencing it. The height of this manoeuvre should be similar to the first.

The model is flown at full throttle along the base line into wind. About two seconds after the call of 'centre', up elevator is smoothly applied. The first quarter of the half loop sets the radius for the entire manoeuvre so remember less elevator may be required in stronger winds. During the second quarter, to adjust for decaying speed and/or the effect of the wind, a reduction in elevator may be required. At the top of the loop the model is held inverted along a horizontal line and almost *immediately* half-rolled to upright.

Use the call of 'centre' to help gauge the timing of the point at which down elevator is smoothly applied to fly the half outside loop. Throttle back as the half-loop is entered. As the model is now flying downwind enough down elevator needs to be applied to achieve the same radius of curve as flown for the first half-loop. As speed increases and the model heads back into wind more down elevator may be required to maintain its shape and ensure the bottom of the loop finishes at the same height as entry. At the bottom of the half-loop the model is held inverted along a horizontal line and almost *immediately* half-rolled to upright.

Throughout the manoeuvre ailerons will be used to keep the wings level and rudder used to keep the model on the correct track. Remember the sense of direction of the rudder changes after each half-roll.

Downgrades

ENTRY AND EXIT LINES:
flightpath not horizontal
absence of entry/exit lines
heading change

wings not level
entry and exit lines at different heights

HALF-LOOPS:
loop not round
radii not constant
heading change
wings not level

HALF-ROLLS:
half roll not axial
heading change
roll rate not consistent
half-rolls do not follow *immediately* after the half loops
under or over-rolled

Half reverse cuban eight

Description

The model pulls up into a 45-degree climb, half-rolls, then executes an inside loop back to level flight.

Caller's contribution

a) Give warning if the end box limits are likely to be exceeded.
b) Call next manoeuvre *slow roll*.

Component parts

1. Horizontal Entry Line (on the *base line*).
2. Eighth Inside Loop to 45-Degree Line Up.
3. Short 45-Degree Line Up.
4. Half-Roll on 45-Degree Line to Inverted.
5. Short 45-Degree Line Up Inverted.
6. Five-Eighths of an Inside Loop to Horizontal Upright.
7. Horizontal Exit Line (on the *base line*).

This manoeuvre should be of a similar size to the first.

The model is flown upwind at full throttle and, at a point approximately

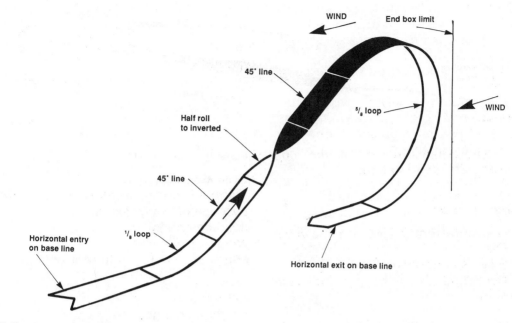

WIND

End box limit

45° line

Half roll
to inverted

5/8 loop

WIND

45° line

Horizontal entry
on base line

1/8 loop

Horizontal exit on base line

Half reverse cuban eight.

midway between the centreline and the box limit, an eighth loop is smoothly pulled so the model tracks a 45-degree line upwards. After a short straight line the model is half-rolled to inverted followed by another short straight line of the same length as the first before up elevator is smoothly applied to pull the model into a five-eighths loop to exit the normal way up on the base line.

Throughout the manoeuvre the ailerons will be used to keep the wings level and rudder used to keep the model on track.

Downgrades

ENTRY AND EXIT LINES:
flightpath not horizontal
absence of entry/exit lines
heading change
wings not level
entry and exit lines at different heights

LOOP SECTIONS:
radii not constant

loops not round
heading change
wings not level

SHORT 45-DEGREE LINES:
flightpath not at 45 degrees
heading change
wings not level
not of equal length

HALF-ROLL:
half-roll not axial
heading change
roll rate not consistent
under or over-rolled

Slow roll

Description

The model rolls slowly through one complete revolution in either direction.

Caller's contribution

a) Call *centre* as the model passes the centreline.

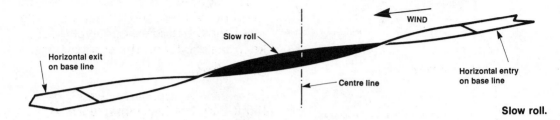

Slow roll.

b) Call next manoeuvre *half square loop with half-roll in upline*.

Component parts

1. Horizontal Entry Line (on the *base line*).
2. Slow Roll Horizontal.
3. Horizontal Exit Line (on the *base line*).

The model is flown at full throttle downwind and, at a point approximately midway between the box limit and the centreline, a slow roll is initiated. Remember that during the slow roll, elevator and rudder need to be alternately applied to ensure the model maintains a straight track at a constant height. The rate of roll must be consistent throughout. At the call of 'centre' the model should be at an attitude which is midway between inverted and knife edge flight.

During the first quarter of the roll as the model approaches knife edge flight, progressively apply rudder in the opposite direction of the roll (ie. if rolling to the right apply left rudder). As the model approaches inverted, ease off the rudder and introduce enough down elevator to maintain a constant height. As the model approaches knife edge again, elevator is eased off and rudder is applied but this time in the same direction as the roll (ie. if rolling to the right apply right rudder). As the model approaches upright, neutralise the controls to maintain level upright flight.

Downgrades

ENTRY AND EXIT LINES:
flightpath not horizontal
absence of entry/exit lines
heading change
wings not level
entry/exit lines at different heights

SLOW ROLL:
roll not axial
heading change
roll rate not consistent
roll less than four seconds
roll not central to the centreline
roll does not rotate through 360 degrees

Half square loop with half roll in upline

Description

The model pulls through a quarter-loop into a vertical attitude, executes a half-roll in either direction, then pushes through a quarter outside loop to recover in level flight at a higher altitude than entry.

Caller's contribution

a) Give warning if the end box limit is likely to be exceeded.
b) Call next manoeuvre *three turn spin*.

Component parts

1. Horizontal Entry Line (on the *base line*).
2. Quarter Inside Loop to Vertical Line Up.

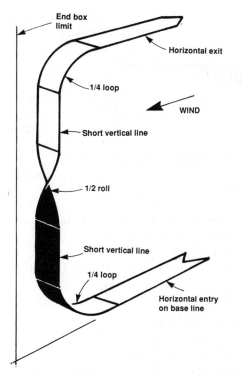

Half square loop with half roll in upline.

3. Short Vertical Line Up.
4. Half-Roll in Vertical Upline.
5. Short Vertical Line Up.
6. Quarter Outside Loop to Horizontal Upright.
7. Horizontal Exit Line (on the *top line*).

Bear in mind that the next manoeuvre is a three-turn spin so the model needs to exit from this manoeuvre with sufficient height to allow room for recovery from the last three turn spin.

The model is flown downwind at full throttle within the limit of the box and up elevator is smoothly applied to take the model into a vertical climb. After a short pause the model is half-rolled and the vertical line continued for the same distance as the first before smoothly applying down elevator to push the model into a quarter-loop of the same radius as the first. The model exits upright on the top line.

Throughout the manoeuvre the ailerons will be used to keep the wings level and the rudder and elevator used to keep the model on the correct track.

Downgrades

ENTRY, SHORT VERTICAL AND EXIT LINES:
flight path not horizontal/vertical
absence of entry/exit lines
heading change
wings not level
short vertical lines not equal

HALF-ROLL:
roll not axial
heading change
roll rate not consistent
under or over-rolled

QUARTER-LOOPS:
radii not consistent
loops not round
heading change
wings not level

GENERAL:
half-loop not square

Three turn spin

Description

The model establishes a heading, power is reduced, the model is held in a slightly nose high attitude until it stalls and commences to spin. The model will autorotate through three complete spin turns and recover on the same heading but at a different altitude.

Caller's contribution

a) Count the model into the centre, ie. *5—4—3—2—1—centre* (note the caller must take account of the slowing of the model and gauge the countdown to ensure the *centre* call coincides with the centreline. At the same time the pilot must throttle

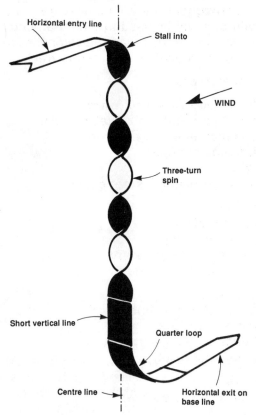

Labels on diagram:
Horizontal entry line
Stall into
WIND
Three-turn spin
Short vertical line
Quarter loop
Centre line
Horizontal exit on base line

Three turn spin.

countdown to the centre and try to time the slowing of the model so that it stalls as near the call of 'centre' as possible. The caller may need a little practice to be able to judge the timing of this countdown call. At the stall the nose will drop, as will one wing, and it is in the direction of the lower wing that the model should spin. Use aileron elevator and rudder to keep the model spinning down a vertical line. After about two and a half spins, neutralise (let go of) the sticks and the model should stop rotating with the canopy facing upwind. Continue the vertical descent for a short moment before smoothly applying up elevator to pull a quarter-loop to exit upwind along the base line.

Downgrades

ENTRY, SHORT VERTICAL AND EXIT LINES:
flightpath not horizontal/vertical
absence of entry/exit lines
heading change
wings not level
does not finish on the same heading

STALL:
did not stall or snap rolled into the spin
(spiral dive scores *zero*)

THREE SPINS:
did not make three turns

QUARTER-LOOP:
radii not constant
loop not round
heading change
wings not level

If the initial entry to a spin is not smooth or the spin itself is jerky and uncertain this is *not* a reason for downgrading, it is an indication that the spin is a true spin.

A *spiral dive* is indicated by its *smoothness* and *increasing airspeed*; during a true spin the airspeed does not increase appreciably.

back in accordance with the countdown to ensure the model stalls as near the *centre* as possible.

Component parts

1. Horizontal Entry Line (on the *top line*).
2. Stall.
3. Three Turn Spin on Vertical Downline.
4. Short Vertical Line Down.
5. Quarter Inside Loop to Horizontal.
6. Horizontal Exit Line (on the *base line*).

The model flies into wind along the top line using ailerons to keep the wings level. Reduce the throttle to idle and at the same time gradually apply up elevator to keep the model at a constant height with its nose up. Listen for the

Chapter 8
At a competition

DETAILS of centralised competitions controlled by the BMFA are listed in most of the radio control model magazines and those for the GBRCAA are via their own newsletters.

Competitions do not run themselves and the Contest Director (CD) has quite a lot on his plate. To help ensure they run smoothly there are several things entrants can do to help.

1. File the entry form with any entry fees as soon as possible, usually at least two weeks before the competition date.
2. Arrive in plenty of time, assemble your model, register your arrival and attend the pilots' briefing. Any queries about the competition should be raised at this time and not once the contest is in progress.
3. Make sure that your insurance and membership are valid and carry documentary proof with you. Follow the rules for transmitter control.
4. Some competitions take place on military airfields and it is essential that local rules about use of camera equipment, clearing up the runways, etc., are strictly adhered to.
5. Be prepared to take a turn in scribing for the judges, volunteer rather than wait to be asked. There may be other tasks such as collecting results slips or totting up marks, and the CD will be most grateful for any help.
6. Whatever your placing do always try and wait until the prize giving has been completed before you leave.

For personal comfort make sure you have suitable clothing. Flying sites tend to be exposed places and windproof/ waterproof anoraks are usually a must, even in summer. Food usually follows bring-your-own-picnic lines but some local clubs are able to put on a barbecue or similar. Apart from major events there are rarely any toilet facilities other than trees or long grass!

Judging

This is probably the most moaned-about aspect of any competition, especially where the judging has to be subjective as in ice-skating and pairs swimming.

The judges all go through a period of training but nevertheless during any flight by any individual a mistake could be made either to the detriment or benefit of the pilot. To minimise the possibility of this happening there are usually several judges and the top and bottom scores are discounted and the remaining scores averaged. Despite this, seldom will a competition go by without someone feeling they have been unfairly marked. Please accept that the judges are doing their best to ensure a fair competition and that their decision is final. If there is a genuine grievance the matter should be raised with the GBRCAA Chief Judge, but outside the competition.

The principles of judging are based on the perfection with which the model simulates full-scale aircraft performance. Thus the precision of the manoeuvre, its positioning, size of dimensions and smoothness/gracefulness are taken into account in that order of importance.

Precision

Just prior to the entry of a manoeuvre the judge will form an image of the course the model will follow. Here a properly defined horizontal entry line is so important. If the first part of the manoeuvre is smaller or larger than that which the judge assumed, he will adjust his image accordingly and thereafter watch to see how far the rest of the manoeuvre accords with this base line. A properly defined horizontal exit line concludes the manoeuvre.

Positioning

Judges invariably sit just behind the pilot and manoeuvres must be positioned

Pilot and caller with judges seated behind.
(Photo: A. Nicholls)

so they can be easily seen. Judges are aware that flying defects can be disguised by flying at a distance beyond the 150 metre line, and downgrades, even though a manoeuvre may otherwise be fine, will be made for flying too far out. Flying too close in will also be downgraded.

Manoeuvres are flown as either End or Centre manoeuvres. End manoeuvres must not exceed box limits nor should they be flown too close to the centre. Centre manoeuvres must be central over the centreline. The base line must be of a reasonable height and constant throughout the flight. Looping manoeuvres must be executed in a plane perpendicular to the line of sight of the model.

Size of manoeuvre

The optimum size of a manoeuvre within the limits of the box is governed by the performance of the model. Avoid small, tight manoeuvres with unnecessarily high rates of roll, pitch and yaw. Use as much of the space within the limits of the box as possible and try to present a flight in which the size of the manoeuvres are in proportion to each other.

Smoothness/gracefulness

These relate to full-scale simulation and the effects of the manoeuvre on the imaginary pilot in a full-scale aircraft.

The keyword is *constant* for the rate of roll, radii of loops, and speed. Any sudden jerks or twitchiness which are considered in excess of full-scale tolerance will be downgraded. A constant speed may be very difficult to achieve but powering through every manoeuvre can hardly be considered graceful.

The 1 Point/15 Degree rule

The 1 Point/15 Degree rule provides a general rule for downgrading deviations from defined manoeuvre geometry. One point is deducted for each approximate 15-degree deviation. Lines are, in general, judged more critically than deviations in yaw or roll.

With an inverted engine a model stand is invaluable for maintenance and ease of starting.
(Photo: A. Nicholls)

Noise testing. *(Photo: A. Nicholls)*

Individual manoeuvres

The rule for the judges is 'when in doubt give the lower score'. Each manoeuvre starts with ten points from which deductions or downgrades are made depending on how far the manoeuvre fails to adhere to what is described for that manoeuvre in the F3A rules. The reasons for downgrading are:

1. the number of defects observed.
2. the severity of the individual defects.
3. the number of times any one defect occurs.
4. the positioning of the manoeuvre.
5. the size of the manoeuvre.

Two examples of how a score *may* be arrived at

1. A Half Reverse Cuban Eight is started too late and the pilot squeezes the manoeuvre by flying a 60-degree line (instead of 45 degrees) and is unable to fit in a straight line between the half-roll and the ⅛ loop to exit on the horizontal line. The manoeuvre goes halfway outside the box limit.

Deduct 1 point for the 60-degree angle, 2 points for omitting the line after the half-roll and 3 points for going out of the zone. Score is 4 points out of a possible 10.

2. Three Inside Loops are entered in a slight climb. The first circle is central and of constant radius, the second suffers a 15-degree dropped wing and a tightened second half and the third is entered late (20 degrees off-centre) and is not symmetrical. The exit from the manoeuvre is at a different height from the initial entry. After the first circle the attempt made by the pilot to correct the dropping wing, loss of symmetry, etc., causes the manoeuvre to appear rushed and jerky.

Deduct 1 point for the climb on entry, 1 point for the dropping wing, 1 point for the lack of symmetry in the second loop, 1 point for the third circle being off-centre, 1 point for the lack of symmetry of the third circle, 1 point for the exit at a different height and 1 point for lack of smoothness/ grace. Score is 4 points out of a possible 10.

Appendix 1
The control model

IN ORDER to prove the content of this book and to make sure it was of use to newcomers to aerobatics, the authors commissioned Millers Radio Models to build them a standard, off-the-shelf, low-priced aerobatic type model, and equip it with a standard unpumped engine, normal silencer and a basic radio using standard servos. The idea was to invite a pilot who wished to try aerobatic flying to use this model in conjunction with the first draft of this book to test its relevance and suitability. The comments made by the pilot were then fed into the final version of this book.

MODEL:
Mick Reeves GANGSTER 63
Undercarriage—fixed
Covering—Solarfilm
Adhesive Trim—Decorfilm
Control
    —closed loop to rudder
    —Y-rods to elevator
    —single servo serving both ailerons
Dihedral
    —wings joined flat inverted

Angle of incidence
    (main wing)—1.25 degrees
    (tail plane)—zero degrees
Centre of Gravity
    —110 mm (4¼ inches from the leading edge wing measured along the fuselage
Weight (without fuel)
    —2.62 kilos (5lbs 12ozs)
Throws
    —rudder 50mm each way
    —elevator 6mm up, 7mm down
    —aileron 9mm up, 7mm down

ENGINE:
ENYA 60 Mk 2
sidethrust—three degrees
downthrust—one degree
propeller—Graupner 11 × 7.5
fuel—15% Dynaglow

RADIO:
Futaba Challenger
Servos—standard 148s throughout

General impression

The Gangster is a proven model and very little was needed in the way of trimming to enable reasonably accurate aerobatics to be performed.

The wings were laterally balanced before the first flight and needed no adjustment during the trimming process.

Although the downthrust built into the model was correct, the trimming flights showed that the model pulled to the left in vertical climbs and so the right thrust was increased to three degrees. Packing was placed behind the engine mount at the flying site, and was later made good at home.

It was found necessary to use differential movement on the elevator to give more down throw than up to enable an equal 'feel' of response for inside and outside manoeuvres. Elevator throw was adjusted so fully flaired landings could be achieved, while retaining a soft but adequate control during manoeuvres.

The aileron throw was adjusted to produce a crisp but not over-responsive control.

The model showed very little roll couple when rudder was used indicating a correct dihedral angle.

The engine was a ready starter and adequate for the flights made in calm conditions. It was possible to fly the full schedule with acceptable size manoeuvres but it did struggle a little at the top of extended verticals.

The radio was adequate and the standard servos performed well.

Conclusion

It is feasible and practical to begin competing in the Standard Schedule aerobatics just using basic, well set-up equipment. The accent must be on building a sound and true model and taking time to trim it out. To perform larger, more constant speed manoeuvres, especially in windier weather, a more powerful motor, possibly pumped and/or fitted with a tuned pipe would probably be required.

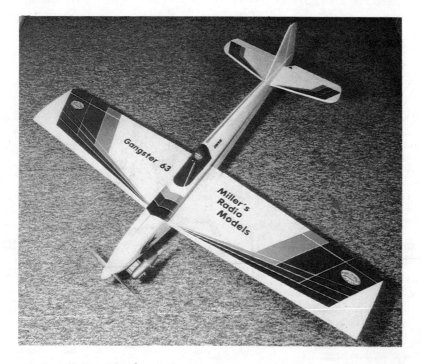

The Gangster 63 **used as the control model.**
(Photo: Tim Allison)

Appendix 2   The current FAI programme (Master Schedule)

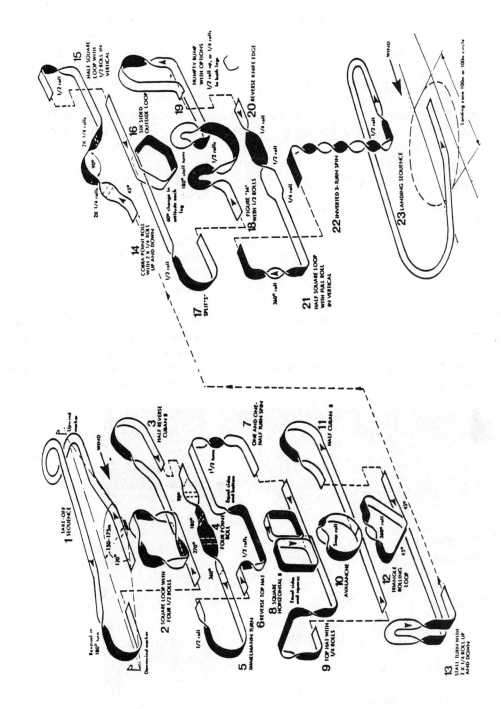

61

Appendix 3
Manufacturers' and suppliers' addresses

Great Britain

British Model Flying Association,
Society of Model Aeronautical
Engineering, Kimberley House,
47 Vaughan Way, Leicester, LE1 4SG
Tel: (0533) 440028

Calypso Models, 17 Davygate Centre,
York, YO1 2SU
Tel: (0904) 634281

Chart Hobby Distributors Ltd.,
Chart House, Station Road, East
Preston, Littlehampton, West Sussex,
BN16 3AG
Tel: (0903) 773170

Irvine Engines Ltd., Unit 2, Brunswick
Industrial Park, Brunswick Way, New
Southgate, London, N11 1JL
Tel: (081) 361 1123

Macgregor Industries Ltd., Canal Estate,
Langley, Berkshire, SL3 6ED
Tel: (0753) 42251

Marvic Models, 16 Rowan Avenue, New
Earswick, York, YO3 8AT
Tel: (0904) 765912

Modeland
219 New North Road, Hainault, Essex.
Tel: (081) 500 3891

J Perkins (Distribution),
90-96 Greenwich High Road, London,
SE10 8JE
Tel: (081) 692 2451

Ripmax Models Ltd., Ripmax Corner,
Green Street, Enfield, Middlesex,
EN3 7SJ
Tel: (081) 804 8272

Dave Smith Models, 59 Newton Road,
Great Ayton, North Yorkshire,
Tel: (0642) 723025

United States of America

Byron Originals Inc., P O Box 279,
Ida Grove, IA 51445
Tel: (712) 364 3165

Dremel, Div. Emerson Electric
Company, 4915 21st Street, Racine,
WI 53406
Tel: (414) 554 1390

Du-Bro Products, 480 Bonmer Road,
Wauconda, IL 60084
Tel: (312) 526 2136

Dynathrust Props Inc., Box 91,
Georgetown, TN 37336
Tel: (615) 476 2330

Futaba Corporation of America,
4 Studebaker, Irvine, CA 92718
Tel: (714) 455 9888

Hobby Lobby International Inc.,
5614 Franklin Pike Circle, Brentwood,
TN 37027
Tel: (615) 373 1444

J'Tec, 164 School Street, Daly City,
CA 94014
Tel: (415) 756 3400

Model Rectifier Corporation (MRC),
200 Carter Drive, Edison, NJ 08817
Tel: (201) 248 0400

Rhom Products Manufacturing
Company, 908 65th Street, Brooklyn,
NY 11219
Tel: (718) 833 4842

Sig Manufacturing Company Inc.,
401–7 South Front Street, Montezuma,
IA 50171
Tel: (515) 623 5154

Sullivan Products, 1 North Haven
Street, P O Box 5166, Baltimore,
MD 21224
Tel: (301) 732 3500